WITHDRAWN

D1469816

DATE DUE

Dogs Helping Kids with Feelings

Terry Vinocur, LCSW

The Rosen Publishing Group's
PowerKids Press ™
New York

Special thanks to all Delta Society pets for the never-ending love they offer to those in need.

Published in 1999 by The Rosen Publishing Group, Inc.
29 East 21st Street, New York, NY 10010

First Edition

Book Design: Michael de Guzman

Photo Illustrations: All photo illustrations by Bonnie Rothstein Brewer.

Vinocur, Terry.
    Dogs helping kids with feelings /by Terry Vinocur.
        p.   cm. — (Dogs helping people)
    Includes index.
    Summary: Describes what Brooke and Sarah, two therapy dogs, do as they help young people work out their feelings in psychotherapy.
    ISBN 0-8239-5214-2
    1. Dogs—Therapeutic use—Juvenile literature. 2.Child psychotherapy—Juvenile literature.
    3. Dogs—Psychological aspects—Juvenile literature. 4. Dogs—Training—Juvenile literature.
    5. Human-animal relationships—Juvenile literature. [1. Dogs—Training. 2. Human-animal relationships.]
    I. Title. II. Series.
RJ505.P47V56   1998
618.92'8914—dc21
                                      98-9263
                                        CIP
                                        AC

Manufactured in the United States of America

Contents

Brooke

Brooke is a breed of dog called a boxer. She has big brown eyes and a tail that moves her whole bottom when she wags it. She is a **therapy** (THER-uh-pee) dog. Brooke works with a woman named Terry. Terry is a **child therapist** (CHYLD THER-uh-pist). Together, they help children and parents understand their feelings. Brooke and Terry help children understand why they might be worried, sad, angry, or confused about things. Sometimes it's hard to live with some feelings. It can help to talk about these feelings with someone who understands.

◁ *Terry and Brooke have been working together for about four years.*

5

Sarah

Brooke and Terry also have a boxer puppy named Sarah. Sarah is learning how to be a therapy dog just like Brooke. Both Terry and Brooke will teach her the job. Sarah is a young puppy who wants to run, jump, and play. But soon she will learn to sit, stay, and **behave** (be-HAYV). A therapy dog has a very special job, so she learns her job through special training.

Sarah trusts Terry and wants to do a good job for her and Brooke. ▷

Socialization

Puppies need to spend time with many different people so they will be **comfortable** (KUMF-ter-bul) with everyone. This is called **socialization** (SOH-shul-ih-ZAY-shun). It is an important part of Sarah's training. Terry takes Sarah to the shopping mall so she can meet people. Inside the mall Terry sits on a bench near Sarah. There are many new things for Sarah to see, smell, and hear. But most important, there are a lot of people. They ask if they may pet the puppy. Sarah meets men, women, boys, and girls of all ages and sizes.

◁ *Sarah is friendly and gentle with everyone, especially kids.*

Special Dog Training

Another part of Sarah's training is to go to dog school to learn how to behave. Brooke went to dog school too. Every two years Brooke has to take a test with the Delta Society to make sure she can still be a therapy dog. The Delta Society teaches people like therapists how to train their dogs to be therapy dogs. In the test, Brooke walks up to people in wheelchairs. She has to sit, stay, and be calm for three minutes. These can be hard things for a dog to do. But Brooke passes the test each time. When she is ready, Sarah will take this test too.

To prepare for her test, Sarah ▷
practices how to sit and stay.

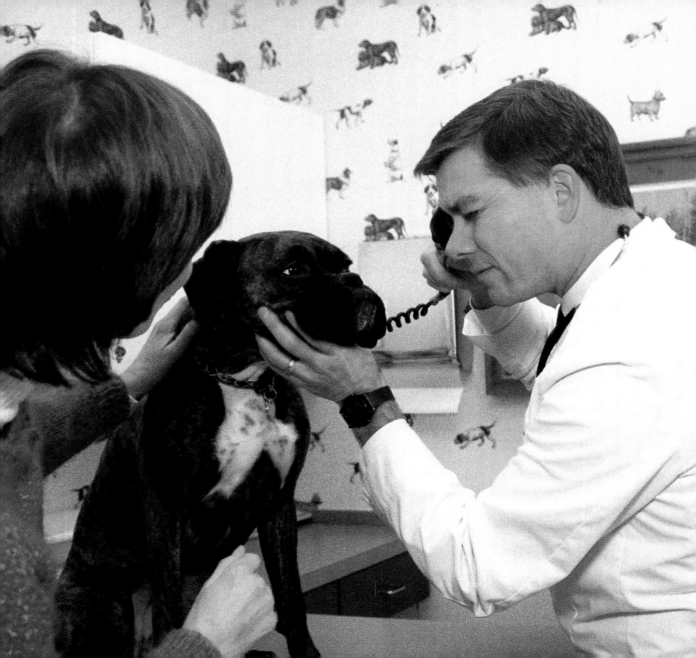

Dr. Goodman

Many animals don't like to go to the **veterinarian** (VEH-tuh-ruh-NAYR-ee-un). But Brooke and Sarah like to visit their vet, Dr. Goodman. He checks them to make sure they are healthy. Once a year they need shots to protect them from **diseases** (dih-ZEE-zez). Terry also helps the dogs stay healthy by bathing and brushing them. Terry makes sure their toenails are clipped and their teeth are brushed. Brooke and Sarah are always clean for their very important job.

◁ *Brooke tries to be good when Dr. Goodman examines her.*

A Kid's Best Friend

People wonder how Brooke helps children. Most of all, she is friendly, gentle, and kind. Children know she is happy to see them when she gives a child a kiss. This makes the child feel special. Brooke helps children feel safe when she sits beside them in Terry's office during their **appointments** (uh-POYNT-ments). Sometimes Brooke jumps up on the sofa and puts her head in a child's lap. Brooke is cozy, and it feels good to pet her head. She makes everyone feel comfortable.

Sometimes talking to a therapist can be scary. ▷
But dogs like Brooke make it easier.

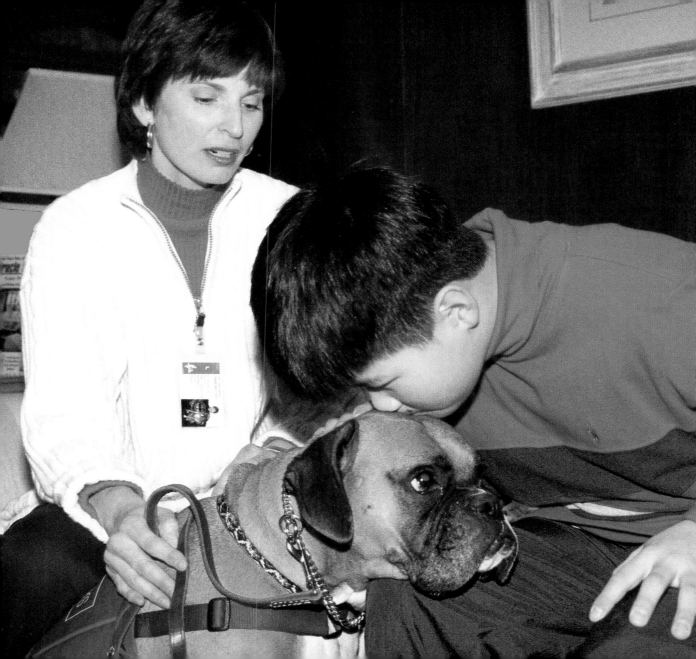

Hugs Can Help

One day an eight-year-old boy told Brooke and Terry some of his feelings about his parents' **divorce** (dih-VORS). He cried when he talked about how much his parents had argued. Brooke helped him by licking his hand. The boy was sad because he would not be able to live with both of his parents anymore. He put his arms around Brooke's neck and hugged her. It was almost as if Brooke gave him a hug too.

◁ Brooke seems to know that just holding and petting her can make a sad kid feel better.

The Operation

A little girl came to Terry and Brooke's office for help. She needed an **operation** (OP-er-AY-shun), and she was scared and worried. Terry told her about an operation that Brooke had on her head. Terry showed her the scar on Brooke's head. Terry explained how the bright green bandages that Brooke wore after her operation helped her get better. The girl decided it would help if she had a green bandage too. She didn't feel so scared after that.

Brooke doesn't mind if kids touch her. She knows she is helping a child to feel ▷ better and understand her feelings.

18

Helping in Other Ways

Brooke and Sarah take naps in Terry's office while Terry talks on the phone or writes notes about her work. Sometimes the dogs go with Terry to meetings with her coworkers. During the meetings Brooke sleeps near Terry's feet. Sarah tries to sit still, but she needs help. She is still learning to behave. The other people in Terry's office smile and pet the dogs. Being with Brooke and Sarah helps Terry's coworkers relax.

◁ *In between appointments, Brooke and Sarah like to take a break from their hard work.*

The End of the Day

When work is done for the day, Terry and the dogs head for home. As she puts them in the car, Terry thanks the dogs for a job well done. At home Brooke and Sarah play and chase each other around the yard for a long time. This is one way the dogs like to relax and have fun after working hard. Sometimes people ask Terry if Brooke likes having a puppy. "Yes," Terry says, "Brooke is happy that Sarah has joined the therapy team." They love their work and each other. Brooke and Sarah are proud to be dogs who help children.

Glossary

appointment (uh-POYNT-ment) A meeting with someone that is planned ahead of time.

behave (be-HAYV) To be well-mannered.

child therapist (CHYLD THER-uh-pist) A person who works especially with children to help them work out their feelings.

comfortable (KUMF-ter-bul) Feeling relaxed and at ease.

disease (dih-ZEEZ) A sickness.

divorce (dih-VORS) The legal ending of a marriage.

operation (OP-er-AY-shun) A way of fixing injury or disease by surgery.

socialization (SOH-shul-ih-ZAY-shun) Helping a person or animal learn to be friendly with many different kinds of people.

therapy (THER-uh-pee) Talking with another person to figure out one's feelings.

veterinarian (VEH-tuh-ruh-NAYR-ee-un) An animal doctor.

Index

24